Anxiety:

How To Cope With Extreme Trepidation and Live Your Life Fully

Table of Content:

Chapter 1 – Trap of anxiety: how it looks, why it appears

...I remember myself having woken up deeply at night. Unable to breathe normally, I could not understand what had happened. I had a strange dream. Particularly, I saw my soul that looked like a young elegant lady who finally set free.

The soul had been flying along the room and felt absolutely delighted. What a forgotten feeling! Then, it heard some bell ordering her to return to the body. Arm, legs and other parts of my organism stifled by numerous depressions could not move. The soul thought: 'Well, this body is so awkward and ill. Perhaps, I need another one to experience this unforgettable moment of freedom and lightness'. Then, I woke up.

My heart was beating absolutely out of the rhythm, with breath out of control. I felt tremendous attacks of panic. Oh my anxiety... How long is it going to affect my life so badly?..

Susan was sitting on the sofa in front of her psychologist. It was not the first time when she visited specialist. Actually, she had to go through the hard times, and help of the well-educated, experienced person who knew the secrets of human heart well came in handy.

The psychologist was aware how to cope with anxiety, panic attacks and shared his opinion:

- *I don't think that you have seen exactly the soul in the dream! Perhaps, you haven't heard about it, however, the soul in the Ancient Greece was considered as another name for state of mind.*

You feel extremely anxious because of deep emotional pain stuck inside. All the emotions which you have tried to suppress started destroying your physical health. The image of freedom which you felt at night was allusion to eagerness to get rid of mental problems and those issues that bother you.

However, in the real life you cannot find solution. Therefore, you body seemed so clumsy. You feel as being completely unable to move forward. The health suffers not because of the medical problem, but because of the real issues.

After the long conversations with psychologists Susan finally confessed. Several years ago she lived through the dark moments in her life. Firstly, her parents were ill, next, the partner left her totally broken, and afterwards, the headaches did not allow working normally and making as big money as she got used to.

Indeed, the unhappiest moments in her life had been left behind. The problems did not seem to grow anymore. Nevertheless, Susan did not have enough courage to start something new, whether it referred to work projects, hobbies, or relationships. She was deeply scared. She did not want to fail again.

Thus, she had chosen an absolutely safe lifestyle with work she really abhorred and casual matches that did not touch her soul at all. During the busy days she looked really confident. However, at dark sleepless nights she appeared in the trap of anxiety.

Well, what does it mean to feel anxious?

The old dictionary is opened. With hand on heart Susan is reading;

'Anxiety is one of the most widespread phenomenon that accompanies clinical symptomatology among people who suffer from neuropsychic and psychosomatic disabilities as well as different psychological problems among healthy people'.

She knew very well that the so-called anxiodepressive syndrome included the rumination of anxiety as well as asthenic feeling being the most typical kind of emotional problems in the psychiatric clinics and the content of the mental illnesses. A great deal of scientists has dedicated their works to the study of that condition.

The intense degree of anxiety makes a destructive effect on the psycho-physiological functions of a person, blocking the effective functioning of mental system.

A person loses the ability to adequately assess the events, analyze the information received, construct a model of the surrounding world that is equal to reality, and make the right decisions. In this case, anxiety is evaluated as a destructive emotional-negative mental state that requires correction.

With anxiety, the cardiovascular system suffers, particularly, the heart rate and blood pressure rise. As well, the activity of the digestive tract is inhibited while the functionality of secretion and peristalsis decreases\. Blood from the digestive tract is redistributed to the muscular system. Thus, the body is preparing for activity.

A wide range of physiological reactions accompanying the state of anxiety explains why a variety of psychosomatic disorders, especially disorders of the gastrointestinal tract and cardiovascular system, are formed against the background of a prolonged state of anxiety.

Even though nowadays the official psychology is quite advanced science, in the terms of mental disturbance, it tries to balance between such two concepts as anxiety and trepidation. he latest is connected with extreme fear and feeling of upcoming danger that might be caused by the possible conditions.

In the meanwhile, anxiety tends to become psychological problem. It appears wherever it wants, not taking into consideration your plans and intentions. For instance, you might be performing at the conference when the heart suddenly starts beating. Even though you are ready for the presentation in front of big audience, the anxiety is out of control.

According to the research made by V.A. Ganzin, long feeling of trepidation is likely to transform into more dangerous forms of anxiety. Therefore, once you have noticed the first signs of such problem, it is necessary to take measures and get to good specialist.

At the same time, famous scientist Charles Spielberger who had invented the scale of anxiety measurement outlined the following peculiarities typical for anxious people:

- *Tendency to perceive a wide range of situations as those that endanger human's self-esteem, respect towards himself and general understanding of prestige;*

- *Inability to react at such problems in a different way apart from the reflection of anxiety.*

If you haven't noticed the serious sigs of anxiety, however, sometimes it is normal for you to experience fear, you might undergo the test of Hanin-Spielberg. It proposes the questions to estimate how you understand the sense of danger.

For instance, be ready to answer the questions how often you are calm, feel that nothing affects your safety badly, as well as experience sadness, happiness and other emotions. Finally, it gives the verdict which is quite close to the real course of actions.

Even though no tests could be foundation to make a diagnosis, it is good to check your mental condition and think about correction, if necessary.

Chapter 2: How anxiety affects our everyday life

The anxiety starts as unpleasant feelings inside. Perhaps, you have just faced numerous problem. Or, maybe, you could not help your closest person. Probably, the one whose opinion is crucially important put a stain of blame on you, and you are unable to demonstrate your innocence. There are a plenty of reasons to feel anxiety.

The modern doctors are ascertained that vegetative nervous system is the one to blame for having anxiety. This part of organism manages the main functions such as blood pressure, and breathing system. Most commonly, the disfunctionality of this system is called vegetative dystonia.

It might be reflected on physical level as orthostatic hypotension, cardiac rhythmic disorders, gastroparesis, impotence, hypohydrosis, and others.

As well, if the nervous system is affected, a person has to deal with somatic diseases, in particular, diabetes, amyloidosis, uremia, systemic diseases, porphyria, alcoholism, etc.

Perhaps, there is no need to explain that the roots of these problems hide in our nerves. Anxiety is the first sign that something has gone astray. Once we have ignored those signs, the health begins its own destruction.

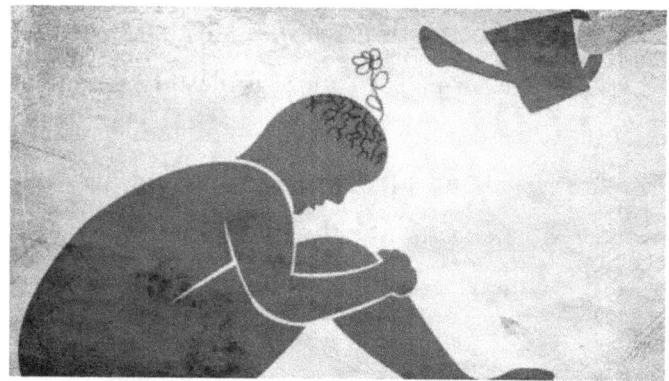

However, the famous psychologist Carl-Gustav Jung proposed different understanding of human anxiety nature. He told that the consciousness of civilized person tries to separate from the primitive instincts. However, they have nowhere to go. They just lost the touch with mind and therefore need to remind about their existence in the form of different illnesses.

Not surprisingly, when the patients visit psychologists for the first time, they give some useful advice. The ill people have to ask themselves many times what the problem speaks with them about.

You have already got familiar with the destiny of Susan. So, when she came to the next specialist, he proposed to visit the psychiatrist and drink some pills. It might sound wonderful, but in a while anxiety disappeared.

However, instead of trepidation, the unbearable headaches started. Susan had been suffering from migraine during one year trying to figure out the best pills ever. Nevertheless, nothing helped you.

After these forlorn attempts, she returned to the first psychologist who recommended her to look deeply inside. The doctor indicated that she had some emotional problem that demonstrated its presence in such a way. As well, the specialist reminded Susan the words of Carl Jung:

- *In case you have depression, why don't you invite this lady in black to the table and start conversation?*

Having come back home, Susan started asking questions what she disliked in her being. During the next week she experienced complete failure at work.

Her partner showed absolute misunderstanding. Susan's parents refused to socialize with her. As well, the trust-worthy friends avoided communication by saying they were busy. Being driven by the desire to get up on the roof and commit suicide, Susan noticed some important thing.

During all this time period she experienced absolutely no headaches. It looked as if the pain that suffocated her came on the surface. Still being angry, Susan was going to say something rude to the psychologist and drove her way to the mental help center when she suddenly bumped into an old friend of hers.

He claimed to have been searching for director's assistant in the theater. He also reminded Susan about her childhood dream to work as an actress. The salary he proposed also seemed quite competitive.

However, the first thought to have in the mind warned:

- *The job position of actress is so unstable! Have you forgotten about your recent business failure? Would you like to receive one more?*

However, Susan asked her friend to give a phone number and headed for psychology center. There, waiting in the queue, she opened the books of Carl Jung and read:

- *A person loves to consider himself as the owner of his sol. However, he is not able to control his mood and emotions which subconsciousness uses to make you act in a proper manner. Therefore, he cannot be regarded as the master of his destiny.*

The modern person protects himself from encountering his own split by creating the system of isolated boxes where he places events happening in his life.

Suddenly, an exciting thought penetrated her mind. The mental system used the tool of anxiety to make Susan go out of the box. She was in danger to get stuck forever. Her emotionality made her harm in order to save her from the trap of the life of complete unfulfillment.

Returning to the theory of Carl Jung, he explained the essence of human soul by illustrating its reflection in such a way. Some alcohol addicted person was influenced by religious movement. Being excited by the enthusiasm of its participants, he totally forgot about drinks. However, the boisterous clergymen used this case acclaiming his wonderful healing thanks to their work efficiency.

Well, in several weeks the novelty of religious ideas seemed less bright for this man, and he drank again. In the meanwhile, his religious benefactors sent him to the mental disabilities hospital.

However, he definitely experienced what we call as anxiety. Trying to get rid of this feeling, he had to drink one bottle after another. But everything he needed was to feel excited.

The modern psychology uses this understanding of anxiety. It looks at different problems, such as depressions, frustration, numerous failures, and inability to create family, lack of desire to build relationships or toxic partnership as the different reflections of anxiety.

Have you ever felt that trembling feeling inside that made you search for some satisfaction in a hurry? Everything starts with anxiety.

Chapter 3: Analytical psychology is a tool to fight with extreme emotions

Analytical psychology of Carl Jung is based on the idea that subconsciousness rules our world. Inside there are the so-called archetypes that affects our life daily.

The behavioral pattern which we follow defines how we act in routine situations and occasions that are important for us. Once a person has figured out his archetype, it becomes easier to explain some actions and, therefore, cope with anxiety. However, let's start with quick test.

Take a sheet of paper and divide it into three columns. It's a good idea to switch on classical music and reach that calm condition which Buddhists called nirvana.

Afterwards, write down in the column the list of abstract words, such as love, hatred, pain, war, caution, childhood, parents, expectations, hope, end, beginning, etc.

Then during ten second try to find out associations that come up to you for the first time. Close your eyes in attempt to clear your mind and afterwards take the second attempt by noting the verbal associations. Then, look through all the concepts you have written down and try to make up sentence with association. Perhaps, it is going to show you where you are heading for.

When Susan did it for the first time, she had such words as 'pain' and 'misery' in front of 'parents'. At the same time, it seemed that 'love' 'hurt' and 'job' is 'boring'.

The whole sentence looked like that: 'When I wake up in the dreary morning, I feel pain because my parents do not understand me. I have a partner whose behavior is equal to the one shown by my parents. I live through abuse and denigration. I am fed up with my work. I used to have some creative ambitious. It seems I wanted to become an actress. However, I feel a deep anxiety when I understand that'.

Finally, we've got that! She wrote down the word 'anxiety' which, actually, disturbed her by continual heart attacks, head spinning, and bad mood with no reason. Her soul was longing for creativity and the test showed the true matter of illness. It has become quite clear why medicine could not help you.

The problem was not connected with physical condition, though. There is even more amazing example of how analytical psychology works. Carl Jung had been treating some patient who suffered because of schizophrenia.

Her relatives vainly begged to save her, however, she was absolutely hopeless, not to mention the fact that official medicine is not able to cure schizophrenia. It only suppresses its symptoms by severe medications.

However, Carl Jung had been working with this woman for a long time giving her abstract tests and trying to take out some secret information from her consciousness. Having analyzed the associations, he got ideas concerning the past of this woman, particularly, some moments in life which he could not remember.It appeared that she used to have a husband and a child.

However, she met a man of her dream and after a short love affair decided to run away from the country with her beloved one. But she did not know what to do with the child whom she loved but was not able to take with her. Thus, she killed a baby. Afterwards, her mental system made a trick with her.

She lived out a terrible trauma, and memory refused to remember at least anything from those days. When Carl Jung had known such fact, he faced a huge dilemma. What if he could talk about that with the woman?

Probably, when the memory returns to her, she would be able to cure quickly? Well, there was anxiety she might commit suicide. He risked, and, surprisingly, the woman got better soon. She recovered her consciousness and lived a life of an adequate person without schizophrenia.

One more aspect of analytical psychology which is also important while working with anxiety is called Shadow. This is the unknown or not so well studied parts of consciousness which include also collective influence.

Trying to figure out the shadow, a person noticed such personality traits which he tried to ignore. It is interesting, by the way, that we usually blame others for what worries us inside, for instance, selfishness, laziness, irresponsibility, and extreme desire to possess.

In some religious practices a person who has noticed reflections of Shadow begins to blame himself. The months go by, but a person might not boast of any real progress in his life. The only thing he has to do is to talk about his spiritual growth.

Actually, the reason of problem is that a person who rejects his Shadow is like the one who does not want to speak with his important side of nature. Instead, he needs to give to the Shadow the ability to demonstrate its better sides.

How to reveal it? Open the copybook and write down the list of things you hate in others. Afterwards, try to come up with the idea how these personality traits are reflected in your own temper. For example, if you hate people who are not generous and consider yourself a giver, think about the situation when you behaved in a mean manner.

Perhaps, it happened with the colleague whom you dislike and therefore did not want to lend him money. Maybe, you were too much immersed into making money process that simply did not notice how another one desperately needed your help.

Having analyzed your behavior, you can get to the next level. The aim of analytical psychology is not to blame and suffer. You, definitely, experience truly negative emotions after this exercise. So, this is time to turn them into better.

Actually, the higher level of anxiety is during the performance, the more prolific task is, too. As far as you have guessed, if your anxiety is able to concentrate fully, you will cope with it quickly.

So, get back to the first list of negative personality traits. Being full of anger and disgust, you need to transform all these bad emotions into productive ones. Thus, in front of each trait describe the situation (real or imaginary) where the stated emotion might do you a favor. For instance, mean person is able to save money for his family.

The main goal of this exercise is to help you manage your feelings. Anxiety itself is not a bad thing. It shows the presence of some imbalance in your life. However, we usually strive to ignore its reflections and think about psychology only when it has started to ruin our bodies and lives completely.

Finally, analytical psychology offers to work with the Shadow (mean, anxiety) by answering one simple question: 'How does my 'bad' personality want to reflect itself?'

For instance, you have seen the presence of cowardly nature. Ask yourself, which character from the book or movie could embody this trait. Then, you need to use your imagination and pretend to be that person for one day (or, if this is too much, for one hour).

Choose the dress, think about your role. Indeed, what will you do? Perhaps, you will go to the forest and then run away? Good sport will lift your spirit, surely. Or, maybe, you are going to the shooting club and train at same time imagining how you kill all the obstacles that can't give you possibility to live full life.

In case you have considered yourself to be lazy, try to act as the magician who makes all the dreams come true by doing nothing. Dress like a wizard, choose an appropriate music (or, perhaps, recall the forgotten musical instruments theory) and organize a funny party.

Or you might go to the garden when nobody is going to disturb you and write down fairy-tale or do anything else which others consider as not serious enough.

Such practices are amazing when you try to cope with anxiety. They will make you feel better and tell you're a bit about the hidden personality you keep inside.

Chapter 4: Metaphorical cards will show the root of the problem

Anxiety traces back to the lost moments of life. We talk about the time periods when instead of crying your eyes out, you ordered yourself to be strong and went straight ahead. At least, you were convinced that you did it.

It started when you decided to think reasonably and rejected from your favorite creative activity because your well-paid work took toll. You have made a choice in favor of something considered by the majority of people as proper and wise, however, you have never confirmed to be feeling completely unhappy.

No wonder, anxiety has something to do with the roots of subconsciousness. To find out why the problem appeared, you need to look at its eyes.

Visual effect would help you to reach the purpose.The modern psychology, along with numerous associations activities, mindmaps, and free drawing techniques, has invented such amazing tool to cope with anxiety as metaphorical cards.

In the middle 1970s Canadian professor Ely Raman tried art therapy while working with hidden desires and concealed pain. He thought that art should serve not for the purpose to become a masterpiece, but give pleasure and satisfaction to the person who tries his hand out. He created a set of things called 'OH cards' using derived word from the exclamation of astonishment.

The cards combination was intended to evoke the logical assumptions and emotional reaction. Since then, this psychological tool has become extremely popular, especially when one needs to cope with anxiety.

Apart from the reason indicated before when a person experiences anxiety as the reflection of his hidden desires, there is one more explanation. Our subconsciousness understands the language of pictures.

Let all the scientists argue if 'the Universe hears the particle NOT', it does not make any sense. Once we have seen some picture, and it appeared to be quite eye-catching, we might follow this behavior pattern throughout our lives.

For example, some woman went to the village and saw how pigs have been slaughtered. She was shocked looking how the poor animal suffered, and came to conclusion not to try meat anymore. Indeed, if the decision is wisely applied, it sounds good, however, it was made under a deep influence of negative subconscious emotions.

In the same way, if a child saw how his parents were fighting with each other, strange thing happens with his mind. He experiences severe anxiety and, perhaps, inability to cope with problems being adult because he could not separate the image of arguing parents from his own personality. For him it means that he had been hit.

So, in such a way the task of psychologist is to show that other people's problems should not affect his life as he has his own decisions, goals and desires. In case of the second reason of anxiety, metaphorical cards will help to change the negative experience onto positive pictures.

How to work with them?

Metaphorical cards might be bought in the store, played online or even made on your own. They represent abstract things which might cause different emotions depending on the type of problem. To reach a good result, it is necessary to involve all your senses and get to the bottom of your consciousness.

For that purpose, you need a set of cards, some sheets of paper, various genre music and, of course, desire to find the root of the problem. Believe me; you will do it sooner or later.

The classical game proposes to take one card out and answer the questions: 'What does it mean for me? Which emotions do I feel looking at it? Where might I find myself on the picture? What is the story about, how it started and finished?'

Choose the music you like (however, you had better not choose too emotional sounds, opt for classical pieces to calm down your mind) and start writing. You might note down all the thought that come to you while answering the mentioned questions. In 15-20 minutes stop this activity and break the ritual.

What does it mean? Every process conducted with subconsciousness requires accompanying elements. Music is the tool, beautiful pencils which you use for writing are good. So, to return to the normal state of mind, drink a glass of water or do some household chores.

It is necessary to repeat this activity during two weeks, only after that you are allowed to read the notices you have made. Stay assured, you will figure out a great deal of interesting things there?

When Susan tried metaphorical cards, she took the one with the images that resembled silent street in the dark evening with the only silhouette. Even though it might be associated with the unlimited space of possibilities for one person, Susan saw the deep loneliness in it. This is how metaphorical cards showed her some routine problem.

When she was alone, she never tried to find some solution or even do something creative. Instead, she was involved into the ruminations. Having tried the second technique when she needed to choose three best cards from the set, Susan opted for the ones that showed some kinds of violence (or, at least, could be interpreted like that).

This is how she recalled that parents might hit her in the childhood if she did not bring good marks. Then, it turned to such an awful fear of failure that every problem made her distract from life completely and immerse into totally safe activities refusing from the satisfaction of life. At this point, it is very important, also, to write about your emotions.

In case you have just worked with cards, the feelings might become so overwhelming that it could be hard to cope with them. However, once you have written them down, it gives you a hint where the problem hides and what to do with it.

If you like pictures and think that metaphorical cards are good for you, try other ways;

- *Look at five cards and think what is missing at each picture to add the story of your life;*

- *Put seven cards in front of you and try to find similarity between your temper and what has been depicted here. For example, I am as patient as this doctor;*

- *Take some card which is going to represent your problem. Speak with it as if you might socialize with the real person (this technique aims at separation of a person from the problem);*

- *The cards represent all the possibilities of your dream life. Take a big sheet of paper and put all the cards which you find necessary. You might add all the subjects which serve good for you. Afterwards, write down which feelings you have got and to which conclusions you have come after completing this exercise.*

Chapter 5:NLP as the way to clear your thoughts

Neuro-linguistic programming is the boundless source for inspiration for people who have absolutely differently problems. It helps to solve the questions of toxic relationships, find the right partner, and make good money. Generally, NLP works with the assumptions and beliefs that limit us in our development. It helps to clear the mind from all the rubbish which we get day by day.

To use its methods and cope with anxiety, there is an amazing tool. As a matter of fact, anxiety affects all the areas of our life badly. Everything we want is just to huddle oneself up in a corner and hide from all the people around us. So, this is time to move out of the box!

The following NLP practice will help you to get rid of anxiety, fill your life with only positive pictures and, finally, make your dreams come true.

The whole practice involves five-day activities and concentrates on the work with our senses. Have you ever noticed that being anxious it is hard for us to get into this reality? Perhaps, you even feel a bit sleepy all the time, so, this is the right moment to awaken your personality!

Each day needs to be dedicated to one organ of senses. It might be illustrated by the following example. On Monday you live as if you have only eyes, Tuesday is the day of auditory way of life, on Wednesday you might make yourself happy by delicacies and other sweet things that are pleasant for your tastebuds.

On Thursday don't forget to devote yourself to the magical art of touching and feeling this life while Friday is the perfect moment to smell this world.

How does it look like?

The probable program for the following week:

-   *On Monday — you choose the most existing parts and try to see the beauty of nature; then you get to the art gallery and spend some time there. It is important to ask yourself a question what you like here. As well, such a technique is a good way to develop creativity and extend the borders of your imagination. Finally, you might choose the dresses of different colors and look how amazingly they correspond with each other.*

- *On Tuesday – visit the concert of local band! If there is no possibility, listen to your favorite music. This is also a good idea to make a list of music store in your city and get there. As well, you might go for a long walk and listen to the sounds of nature trying to pay more attention to what has been hidden from you recently.*

- *On Wednesday go to several places to try the cuisine of different countries. If it is not possible, prepare for yourself four dishes. One has to have a taste of your childhood, the second is something you are passionate about.*

The third must give you a sense of lightness while the forth needs to be simple yet tasty. This little game is designed to show that all the happy moments (that are usually connected with the time when we were younger) are easy to achieve and repeat.

- *Thursday is the day for hugs. And not only for that! You might go to the fabric shop and touch all the cloth you like. Or you might make a big cleaning up and remain only those things which are pleasant to touch.*

- *On Friday think about your favorite smell! Perhaps, you will find yourself in the niche perfume store looking through the most sophisticated aromas. Smell your coffee and notice which flavor is typical for the world around you.*

Conclusion

Anxiety is the first sign that something has gone astray. People who experience it are often more sensitive than those who have never heard about such feelings.

The most important task of psychologist is to transform the negative emotions into the positive ones. It is a good way to sublimate your anxiety and create something beautiful. Feel happy and enjoy this world!

www.ingramcontent.com/pod-product-compliance
Lightning Source LLC
Chambersburg PA
CBHW070448290526
45791CB00005B/2093